GO TURBO

DISASTERS

KATE SCARBOROUGH

EDGE
FRANKLIN WATTS

LONDON•SYDNEY

Essex County Council Libraries

First published in 2009 by
Franklin Watts
338 Euston Road
London NW1 3BH

Franklin Watts Australia
Level 17/207 Kent Street
Sydney NSW 2000

Copyright © Franklin Watts 2009

Series editor: Adrian Cole
Art director: Jonathan Hair
Design: Blue Paw Design
Picture research: Sophie Hartley
Consultants: Fiona M. Collins and Philippa Hunt,
Roehampton University

A CIP catalogue record for this book is available from the British Library.

ISBN: 978 0 7496 8665 9

Dewey Classification: 904

Acknowledgements:
© Corbis: 8 & 37. © Bettmann/Corbis: 13t & 22b. © Mast Irham/epa/Corbis: 22t. © Michael Reynolds/epa/Corbis: 23. © WEDA/epa/Corbis: 36. © Benjamin Lowy/Corbis: 33b. © Reuters/Corbis: 16. © Vincent Laforet/Pool/Reuters/Corbis: 3 & 19t. © Jim Sugar/Corbis: 35. © Michael S. Yamashita/Corbis: 7tr & 20-21. © Aim Patrice/Corbis Sygma: 38. FEMA photo/Andrea Booher: 6. FEMA photo/Win Henderson: 7tl & 19b. © Robert Paul van Beets - Fotolia.com: Cover (top). Georges Gobet/AFP/Getty Images: 11. Alexander Joe/AFP/Getty Images: 17. John Russell/AFP/Getty Images: 32. Scott Warren/Aurora/Getty Images: 41. Mike Goldwater/Christian Aid/Getty Images: 12. Georges DeKeerle/Getty Images: 15. Sean Gallup/Getty Images: 40. Scott Peterson/Liaison/Getty Images: 14b. George Silk/Time & Life Pictures/Getty Images: 13b. © iStockphoto.com/Can Balcioglu: 30-31. © iStockphoto.com/Shaun Lowe: Cover (bottom). Image courtesy of MODIS Rapid Response Project at NASA/GSFC: 18 & 39. DigitalGlobe/Rex Features: 33t & c. CNRI/Science Photo Library: 9. Gary Hincks/Science Photo Library: 31t. © Shutterstock.com/Andrejs Pidjass: Endpapers. © Shutterstock.com/Julien Grondin: 7 (main). Topfoto: 14t. Courtesy University of Rhode Island: 34

Every attempt has been made to clear copyright. Should there be any inadvertent omission please apply to the publisher for rectification.

Printed in China

Franklin Watts is a division of Hachette Children's Books,
an Hachette UK company.
www.hachette.co.uk

Contents

Words that are highlighted can be found in the glossary.

What is a disaster?

A disaster is an event that causes massive destruction. It can affect many people and cause great loss of life.

People at a relief centre after Hurricane Katrina.

A natural disaster is caused by a natural event, such as a volcano erupting. A man-made disaster, such as a plane crash, happens because of human error or mechanical breakdown.

Floods

Earthquake

A volcano erupting

Look back at the contents page. All of the disasters in this book are 'natural'. What type of disaster do you think is the worst?

Plague

The spread of disease **has caused one of biggest ever natural disasters. From 1300–1400 over 75 million people worldwide were killed by bubonic plague, known as the Black Death.**

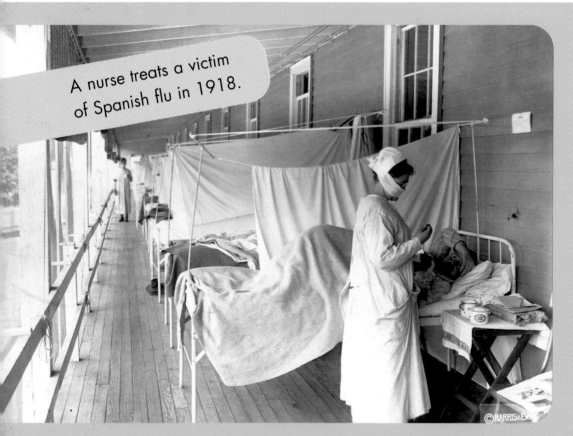

A nurse treats a victim of Spanish flu in 1918.

Spanish flu spread around the globe in 1918, just as the First World War (1914–1918) was ending. It killed up to 100 million people, that's 2–5% of all the people in the world at the time.

Bubonic plague was called the Black Death because sufferers had swollen black spots on their bodies.

These are bubonic plague bacteria, as seen under a powerful **microscope**.

What is a pandemic?

When a disease spreads among people across
a large area, sometimes across the world, the
event is called a pandemic.

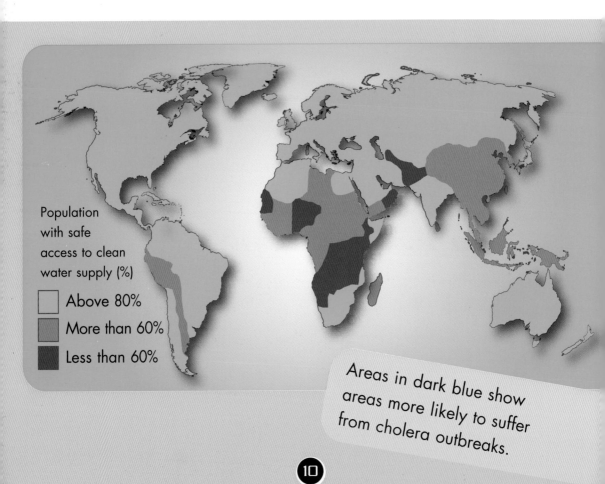

Population
with safe
access to clean
water supply (%)

- ☐ Above 80%
- ☐ More than 60%
- ☐ Less than 60%

Areas in dark blue show areas more likely to suffer from cholera outbreaks.

From 1816 to 1970 there were seven cholera pandemics throughout the world. Cholera gives people terrible stomach cramps and sickness. This can be so bad that it leads to death. Cholera can be caused by drinking dirty water or eating dirty food.

Cholera is still found in poorer countries today.

Go Turbo Life Saver

Cholera and other killer diseases can be treated today. Most people are given special drugs to kill the disease and make them better.

ONLINE//:

www.who.int
Find out more about plague, current health issues and disasters on the World Health Organization's website.

Famine

Famine happens when there is not enough food to feed the number of people who need it. Without help, people can starve to death.

Drought is often the main cause of famine. It affects animals too.

There are many causes of famine:
- crops fail due to bad weather or disease
- there is not enough water to keep the crops alive
- people make poor **decisions**
- people start wars which lead to a food shortage.

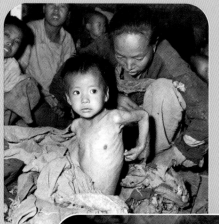

In the Great Famine of China of 1959, 17 to 50 million people starved to death. It was caused by bad weather and people making poor decisions. **?** What might these decisions have been?

In 1984 BBC news reported on a famine taking place in Ethiopia, Africa. The report made a huge impact on viewers. It was one of the first times that people starving to death were shown on TV.

Go Turbo Life Saver

Food aid and money can help to save people. But the causes of famine need to be avoided to stop people starving.

The 1984 famine in Ethiopia became the focus of a massive **fundraising** effort led by Bob Geldof. He gathered together the top singers of the time to make a record called 'Do They Know It's Christmas?' It sold around the world raising money to help those who were dying.

GT Top Fact

Live Aid was a concert organised by Bob Geldof in 1985. He helped to raise over £56 million for the people starving in Ethiopia.

ONLINE//:

www.live8live.com
This is the website of the most recent effort to raise awareness of poverty in Africa – Live 8 – and features case studies and free images.

Floods

When rivers overflow, water floods the land. If there is a lot of water, it has terrible effects. People, animals, buildings and trees are swept away.

Go Turbo Life Saver

Any high point during floods may help to save lives. People climb on roof tops and up trees to stay out of the water. They may be rescued by helicopter.

In 1931, China suffered the worst flood disaster the world has ever known. Heavy rain caused the Yellow River, Yangtze River and Huai River to flood. Up to 4 million people were killed, and over 100 million lost their homes.

These people in Mozambique, Africa are trying to reach safety.

Floods swept through 14 countries in Africa in 2007. Over 2.5 million people lost their animals, homes and crops. They were also at risk from diseases such as cholera, caused by drinking dirty water.

ONLINE//:

http://news.bbc.co.uk/1/hi/world/africa/6994995.stm
Read the BBC's report of the African floods of 2007 on this webpage, which includes a map and videos.

Hurricanes

Hurricanes are also called cyclones or typhoons. They are strong winds that travel at speeds of over 160kph, blowing down trees and ripping off roofs.

GT Top Fact

The **costliest** hurricane in US history hit New Orleans in 2005. Hurricane Katrina caused $81.2 billion's worth of damage.

This is New Orleans after Hurricane Katrina struck.

From July to November every year, big storms cross the Atlantic Ocean from Africa. Some grow in size as they blow towards the Caribbean, Mexico and the USA. Big hurricanes can be 1,000 kilometres (km) across.

ONLINE//:

www.howstuffworks.com/hurricane.htm
There are great videos on this website and storm images, plus find out about how hurricanes behave and see a hurricane's lifecycle.

Earthquakes

Earthquakes are caused by land shifting suddenly. This movement happens in different ways along fault lines. Two sections of land slide, thrust or slip against each other.

GT Record

The top 5 deadliest earthquakes:

1. 1556 Shaanxi, China, estimated 830,000 died
2. 1976 Tangshan, China, 242,000 died
3. 2004 Indian Ocean, 230,000 died
4. 1138 Aleppo, Syria, 230,000 died
5. 1920 Haiyuan, China, 200,000 died.

? What do you notice about some of these places?

Earthquakes occur on three different types of fault:
- A normal fault – one rock face slides down the other
- A thrust fault – rocks push towards each other
- A strike-slip fault – rocks slip sideways against each other.

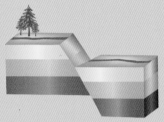
Normal fault

Thrust fault

Strike-slip fault

Earthquakes produce shockwaves, called **seismic waves**, which are measured by scientists using a seismograph.

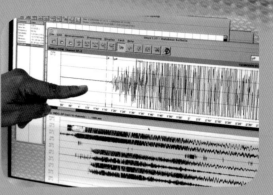

In 1976, Tangshan in China was struck by an earthquake (above). The night before, people had noticed strange lights in the sky. People reported that water in a village well rose and fell three times, and gas escaped from a well in another village.

When an earthquake strikes:
- The ground shakes as the land moves causing buildings and bridges to fall down
- In mountain areas the shaking can also cause **landslides** and avalanches
- Gas pipes can break and fires often start
- If underwater, the earthquake could create a tsunami.

These apartments fell down after an earthquake in Hanwang, China, in 2008.

 Imagine what it is like to be in an earthquake. What would you do? How would you feel?

ONLINE//:

http://earthquake.usgs.gov/learning/kids
This website is from the USGS and is great for finding out about past and present earthquake activity, plus there are puzzles and games!

Fault Line

Written by Leon Read   Illustrated by Kevin Hopgood

I'm on the bus, heading for college on another sunny day in San Francisco. The younger kids are at the front, I'm at the back with my friends Tyreece and Kareem. We're messing around. Kira is a few seats in front, she looks over, gives me a smile. I want to ask her out, but just haven't found the right time.

The bus swerves – feels like a tyre has blown – then the driver hits the brakes. The bus lurches forward at an angle. I grab the seat in front and hang on. The bus slips down into the road before crashing to a stop. Kids start screaming. All I can see out of the window is the road surface and the ground shaking.

"You OK?" I ask Tyreece. He's in shock and just nods. I look up to where Kira was sitting, but now there's just an empty seat. There's broken glass everywhere. Heavy things are crashing on the bus roof. Kareem has a gash over his eye, there's blood on his face.

"Bust open the escape door," I say to Tyreece. He tries the handle but it's jammed, so he swings round and kicks it open. "Come on, let's get everyone out."

"I'll go first," Tyreece says. "Pass them up to me." So I move down the bus, towards the front. Kids are crying. There are bags everywhere.

"Hey, listen up!" I shout. My voice is loud. "The escape door is open at the back, this way." I point up. Kareem reaches down to help people to the back. Tyreece reaches in and pulls them up to the road. I still can't see Kira. Kids are trapped at the front, stuck under seats, stuck under each other. Slowly we move them out.

"Mommy!" some kid cries out, "My arm hurts!" But there's no time for that. I can smell bus fuel. I see Kira, take her hand. She's twisted her ankle or something – can't walk well. So I help her up.

Everyone is out, even the driver who's banged his head. His face is dotted with spots of blood from the flying glass. It's clear what's happened – it was the earthquake we've all been waiting for – all been dreading. The ground has split almost the length of the road. Cars have been left by their drivers, bricks and glass all over the place. Car and shop alarms are screeching.

A medic is treating some of the injured kids. Kareem and Tyreece have rushed home. I'm sitting with Kira.

"So, I never thought it would really happen."

"No way," Kira says. I wrap my jacket around her. She looks at me like she is waiting for me to say something.

"So, are you doing anything at the weekend?" I ask. Kira laughs. "Does it take an earthquake to get you to ask me out? I could have been waiting a long time," she says.

"No, but I just thought..." She puts a finger across my lips. I shut up.

"I'm doing something now – seeing you," she says. Then the ground starts shaking again...

Shifting ground

The ground under our feet may feel solid, but the surface is made up of huge sections called plates.

The plates grind against each other as they move very slowly on top of a layer of hot liquid rock. The movement can cause earthquakes and make volcanoes erupt.

GT Top Fact

San Francisco, USA (below), is built on the San Andreas Fault. The last major earthquake there happened in 1989.

Most global earthquake and volcano activity takes place around the Pacific Ocean. This is known as the 'Pacific Ring of Fire'. It has 75% of the world's volcanoes (red triangles), and 90% of earthquakes (yellow dots).

North America

Australia

South America

ONLINE//:
http://bancroft.berkeley.edu/collections/
earthquakeandfire/splash.html   Visit this website to see
photographs following the 1906 earthquake in San Francisco, USA.

Tsunamis

Tsunamis are huge sea waves that are caused by underwater earthquakes.

On 26th December 2004, an earthquake under the Indian Ocean created a tsunami that **devastated** shorelines in Thailand, Indonesia, India and Sri Lanka. Over 230,000 people were killed.

Go Turbo Eyewitness

"We were still in bed in a ground floor room… when water started coming under the door. Within a few seconds it was touching the window. We scrambled to get out as the windows started to cave in and glass shattered everywhere. We swam out of the room… and up into a tree." *Roland Buerk, tsunami survivor.*

The city of Banda Aceh, Indonesia before (above) and after (below) the tsunami struck.

The devastated shoreline in Banda Aceh after the tsunami.

ONLINE//:

http://edition.cnn.com/SPECIALS/2004/tsunami.disaster
This CNN webpage has lots of information and stories from the tsunami of 2004. (Advisory: includes some scenes of devastation.)

Volcanoes

A volcano is a mountain that erupts molten rock. The largest eruption on record happened in 1815 when Mount Tambora in Indonesia exploded, killing 71,000 people.

These scientists are uncovering the site of the 1815 eruption.

The Mount Tambora eruption was so huge that clouds of ash blasted into the air. The ash affected weather patterns for the next 12 months. This was called 'The Year without Summer'.

GT Record

When Krakatoa, Indonesia, erupted in 1883 it produced the loudest sound ever recorded. The explosion was heard in Perth, Australia, about 3,110km away, and on the island of Rodrigues near Mauritius, about 5,000km away.

Go Turbo Life Saver

The best way to survive an eruption is to make sure you are far away when it happens!

When a volcano erupts a number of things can happen:

- The volcano explodes with a huge bang
- Hot rocks are thrown into the surrounding area
- Boiling lava flows downhill covering the land
- A hot **pyroclastic flow** rushes downhill
- Hot, deadly gases fill the air.

On 8th May 1902, Mount Pelée erupted (below) and destroyed the city of Saint Pierre, Martinique. Over 30,000 people were killed. The volcano, 6.4km north of the city, ripped open, sending out a burning black ash cloud that reached the city in just one minute. The cloud, called a pyroclastic flow, burned everything in its path.

Go Turbo Eyewitness

"The earth began to tremble, and the sky became dark." *Léon Compere-Léandre, survivor of the Pelée eruption.*

ONLINE//:

http://www.geology.sdsu.edu/how_volcanoes_work/ Pelee.html   Find out more about the devastating explosion of Mount Pelée and read stories of extraordinary escapes here.

Fires

Wildfires and bushfires start in open woodland or brush. **They are started by lightning strikes, by heat from the Sun, or by careless travellers.**

In 1871, a great fire swept through Peshtigo, Winsconsin, USA. It killed up to 2,500 people, destroyed 12 towns and burned over 4,000 square km of forest.

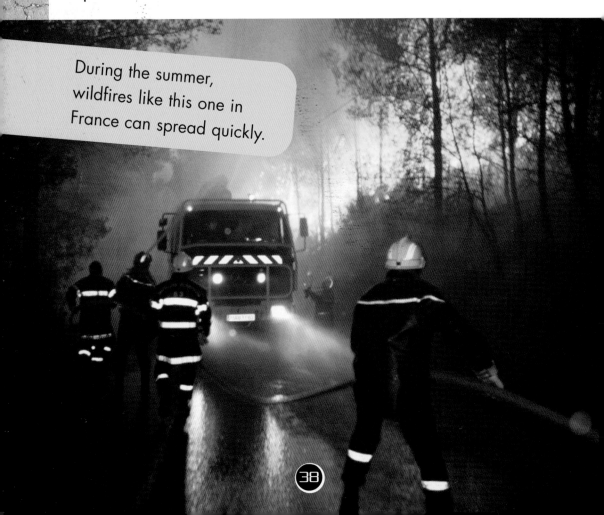

During the summer, wildfires like this one in France can spread quickly.

Go Turbo Eyewitness

"When turning my gaze from the river I chanced to look either to the right or left, before me or upwards, I saw nothing but flames: houses, trees, and the air itself were on fire." *Rev. Peter Pernin, Peshtigo, 1871.*

In February 2009, fires in Victoria, Australia, swept across the dry **bush**. Over 900 homes and more than 3,500 square km of forest were destroyed. Over 200 people were killed.

This is a **satellite** view of southeast Australia showing smoke from bush fires.

ONLINE//:

http://www.rootsweb.ancestry.com/~wioconto/Fire.htm
Find out more about the devastating fire at Peshtigo, including a map of the area, survivors stories and written accounts of the events.

Blizzards and avalanches

Snow might mean fun for most people, but a heavy blizzard could be a disaster. Blizzards are heavy, windy snowstorms that can block roads and trap people.

GT Top Fact

In 1972, a week-long snow blizzard in Iran trapped people in their homes. The freezing cold killed over 4,000 people.

? How do you think you would survive if you were trapped in a car during a blizzard?

Avalanches occur regularly in snowy mountain areas. A wall of ice and snow slides down the mountainside, crushing everything in its path.

An avalanche in the San Juan Mountains, USA.

In 1910, after a nine-day blizzard, the town of Wellington, Washington, USA, was hit by an avalanche. The 3 metre (m) high wall of snow, almost 1km long and 0.5km wide, hit the train station and threw two trains 45m downhill. Nearly 100 people were killed.

ONLINE//:

http://www.edu4hazards.org/avalanche.html
There's an avalanche survival guide on this webpage, including what to pack in your emergency kit. Be prepared, not scared! Includes video links.

Fast facts

The longest earthquake fault rupture (crack in the ground) was created by the Great Sumatran-Andaman earthquake of December 2004. The rupture measured approximately 1200–1300km long.

The longest drought recorded happened in the Atacama Desert in northern Chile. It hardly ever has rain – only a few showers several times a century.

The strongest recorded hurricane since records began happened during October 2005. Hurricane Wilma had wind speeds reaching 270kph.

The spread of a disease called smallpox caused between 300–500 million deaths in the 20th century alone.

In 1921 the greatest snowfall in a single day was recorded. Snow fell to a depth of 193cm at Silver Lake, Colorado, USA.

Answers

These are suggested answers to questions in this book. You may find that you have other answers. Talk about them with your friends. They may have other answers too.

Page 7: This answer will depend on your own choice.

Page 13: The poor decisions included forcing people to work in factories, instead of farming and producing food, and not acting quickly when the food shortage started.

Page 20: Many of them take place in China, whilst the rest are scattered along the Pacific Ring of Fire. (See page 31.)

Page 23: If you are in an earthquake, drop what you are doing, take cover and hold on (Drop, Cover, Hold on). Stay inside away from windows until it is safe. If you are in a car, the driver should slow down and stop. Stay in the car until the shaking stops. You may feel very scared, but try to stay calm and focused.

Page 40: If you are trapped in a car during a blizzard, you would need to be prepared. If there has been a lot of snow or the forecast is bad, make sure you take the following items with you: a mobile phone and a torch to alert others to where you are and to give you light in the dark; extra clothing and blankets for warmth; a candle and some matches for warmth and light; food; a shovel to dig yourself out of trouble and sand to help the wheels gain extra grip on slippery roads.

More websites

For videos, photos, case studies and great facts on a range of natural disasters. You can even recreate your own disaster:

http://environment.natio nalgeographic.com/envir onment/natural-disasters

For facts and the science behind natural disasters:

http://library.thinkquest. org/16132/frames. html

How to be prepared for all kinds of natural disasters. Top tips and hints:

http://www.bt.cdc.gov/ DISASTERS

Find out where today's disasters are taking place and find out how you could help:

www.reliefweb.int

Separate out the facts from the fiction on natural disasters, plus how you can survive them:

www.fema.gov/kids/diz area.htm

Everything you ever wanted to know or ask about tsunamis, and more:

www.ess.washington. edu/tsunami

The top ten of all natural disasters – facts and figures:

http://www.epicdisasters .com

The Global Disaster Alert and Co-ordination System provides real-time updates on current global events and emergencies. Includes maps and archive reports:

http://www.gdacs.org

Glossary

Brush – a thick growth of shrubs and small trees.

Bush – an area of land, often in Africa or Australia, that has few or no settlements.

Costliest – something that is the most expensive.

Decision – a conclusion or judgement reached.

Devastated – ruined or destroyed.

Disease – an illness or sickness caused by either a virus or bacteria.

Drought – a total lack of water or rain in a certain place or area.

Fault line – a break in the Earth's crust along which rocks can shift.

Food aid – food supplied to places during an emergency.

Fundraising – raising money for a particular cause, such as to help survivors of an earthquake.

Kph – short for kilometres per hour, a measurement of distance travelled and the time taken.

Landslide – earth on a slope that suddenly slips down the hill.

Microscope – an instrument used to look at tiny objects by magnifying them greatly.

Overflow – to run over or spill over the banks of a river.

Pyroclastic flow – the flow of hot rocks and gases that escapes from a volcano when it erupts and flows downhill, burning everything in its path.

Satellite – a spacecraft in space that circles the Earth. Some satellites can take images of the Earth.

Seismic waves – the movement caused by ground shifting during an earthquake. The waves can be measured to find out the size and strength of the earthquake.

Index